debbie tucker green

For the Royal Court: *ear for eye*; *a profoundly affectionate, passionate devotion to someone* (-noun); *hang*; *truth and reconciliation*; *random*; *stoning mary*.

Other theatre includes: *nut* (National); *generations* (Young Vic); *trade* (RSC); *born bad* (Hampstead); *dirty butterfly* (Soho).

Film and television includes: *swirl, second coming, random*.

Radio includes: *Assata Shakur: The FBI's Most Wanted Woman* (adaptation); *lament*; *gone*; *random*; *handprint*; *freefall*.

Directing includes: *a profoundly affectionate, passionate devotion to someone* (-noun); *hang*; *nut*; *truth and reconciliation* (all theatre); *second coming* (feature film); *swirl* (short film); *random* (film); *Assata Shakur: The FBI's Most Wanted Woman*; *lament*; *gone*; *random* (all radio).

Awards include: Radio Academy Arias Gold Award (*lament*); International Film Festival Rotterdam Big Screen Award (*second coming*); BAFTA for Best Single Drama (*random*); Black International Film Award for Best UK Film (*random*); OBIE Special Citation Award (*born bad*, New York Soho Rep. production); Olivier Award for Best Newcomer (*born bad*).

debbie tucker green

stoning mary

NICK HERN BOOKS
London
www.nickhernbooks.co.uk

A Nick Hern Book

stoning mary first published in Great Britain in 2005 as a paperback original by Nick Hern Books Limited, The Glasshouse, 49a Goldhawk Road, London W12 8QP

Reprinted with revisions 2018

stoning mary copyright © 2005, 2018 debbie tucker green

debbie tucker green has asserted her right to be identified as the author of this work

Cover image: Lisa Johansson/Research Studios

Typeset by Country Setting, Kingsdown, Kent CT14 8ES
Printed in Great Britain by Mimeo Ltd, Cambridgeshire PE29 6XX

A CIP catalogue record for this book is available from the British Library

ISBN 978 1 85459 856 1

Woodland
CARBON
www.woodlandcarbon.co.uk
NICK HERN BOOKS
Printed on Carbon Captured paper

stoning mary was first performed at the Royal Court Theatre Downstairs, London, on 1 April 2005. The cast was as follows:

WIFE	Emily Joyce
WIFE EGO/OLDER SISTER EGO	Heather Craney
HUSBAND	Peter Sullivan
HUSBAND EGO/BOYFRIEND EGO	Martin Marquez
MUM	Ruth Sheen
DAD	Alan Williams
CHILD SOLDIER	Cole Edwards
OLDER SISTER	Claire Rushbrook
YOUNGER SISTER	Claire-Louise Cordwell
BOYFRIEND	Rick Warden
CORRECTIONS OFFICER	Gary Dunnington

Director	Marianne Elliott
Designer	Ultz
Lighting Designer	Nigel Edwards
Sound Designer	Ian Dickinson

for sam and luke

thanks to ruth little, caryl and maria

Characters

WIFE
WIFE EGO
HUSBAND
HUSBAND EGO
MUM
DAD
CHILD SOLDIER (SON), *his hair shaved down to a number one*
OLDER SISTER
YOUNGER SISTER (MARY)
CORRECTIONS OFFICER
BOYFRIEND
BOYFRIEND EGO
OLDER SISTER EGO

The play is set in the country it is performed in.

All characters are white.

All characters start onstage.

Scene titles to be shown.

Names without dialogue indicate active silences between those characters.

/ marks where dialogue starts to overlap.

During 'The Prescription', two actors play each character simultaneously.

One

'The AIDS Genocide. The Prescription.'

WIFE	'If you'd putcha hands – put your hands on me –
	If you'd put your hands on me then you'd know – '
WIFE EGO	said.
WIFE	'Put your hands on me to know'
WIFE EGO	said
WIFE	'handle me to know'
WIFE EGO	I said
WIFE	'handle me. Handle me – handle me – go on.'
	WIFE *shows her shaking hands.*
	'Go on.
	Go on. See… can't. Putcha hands on / me'
WIFE EGO	he gives it –
HUSBAND	'no.'
WIFE	'Putcha' –
HUSBAND	'no.'
WIFE	'Go on' –
WIFE EGO	says –
HUSBAND	'I know.'
WIFE EGO	Says –

HUSBAND	'I know how to handle'
WIFE EGO	says
HUSBAND	'I know how to handle you. Know how to handle you to know – '
WIFE EGO	asks me –
HUSBAND	'why don'tchu put your hands on me?'
WIFE EGO	Says –
HUSBAND	'why don'tchu put your hands on me then?'
HUSBAND EGO	Eyes to the skies it.
HUSBAND	'Go on, put your hands on me – '
HUSBAND EGO	she eyes to the skies it – focus on the floors it
HUSBAND	'what if I want you to that – or you don't want me to get from you what you want from me…? Put me hands on meself if I wanna feel that. Can get me to feel me to feel that can't I? Or you sayin your shakes is somethin special?'
WIFE EGO	Shows me his hands
HUSBAND	'Anyone can do nervous.'
HUSBAND EGO	Hands in pocket
HUSBAND	'Anyone can do nervous well.'
WIFE EGO	Hands in pockets then –
HUSBAND	'Anyone can play nervous well better'n you'
WIFE EGO	hands in pockets doing defiant – doin defiant badly.
HUSBAND EGO	Why would I wanna put my hands anywhere else?

HUSBAND	'Why would I wanna put my hands on anyone else?
	Why would I wanna put my hands on / you?'
WIFE	'You wouldn't know.'
WIFE EGO	Face off the floor – look him in the eye.
HUSBAND EGO	Looks me in the eye now, now she thinks she got somethin to say
WIFE	'You wouldn't know iss been that long'
HUSBAND	'not long enough'
WIFE	'not long enough – never was'
HUSBAND EGO	liar
WIFE	'was it?'
WIFE EGO	Liar
HUSBAND	'I wouldn't know? Wouldn't wanna know.'
WIFE	'You never did know – did know how, didja… husband?'
HUSBAND	'Didn't I?'
WIFE	'Dontcha.'
HUSBAND	'Put me hands on you to the point you didn't know what to do with yourself didja?… Didja. Wife.'
WIFE	
HUSBAND	
WIFE	'Didn't you think it would be like this?
	' "Till death do us" an' all that – y'didn't think it would be like this didja? Didn't think we'd get to this. Didn't think we'd be doin this. Didn't think we'd get to this

	part. Y'didn't think dyin would draw out so dramatic, didja?'
WIFE EGO	Eyes to the skies it.
	He eyes to the skies it, buyin a breather.
HUSBAND	'Blinked and missed the good bits did I?'
WIFE	'What?'
HUSBAND	'Nuthin.'
WIFE	'What?'
HUSBAND	'Blinked and / missed the – '
WIFE	'Huh?'
HUSBAND	'Nuthin.'
WIFE EGO	Waitin on me to 'what' it again, wantin me to 'what' it again to get his attention –
HUSBAND	
WIFE EGO	but I won't.
WIFE	'You got nuthin to say?'
HUSBAND EGO	
WIFE EGO	He says nothing.
WIFE	'You got nothing to say then?'
HUSBAND	
WIFE EGO	Can't say nuthin
WIFE	'You got nothin to say to me – and don't be lookin away – '
HUSBAND	'what?'
WIFE EGO	I said –
WIFE	'don't be looking – you're doing that – '
HUSBAND	'I'm looking / atcha.'
WIFE	'That thing.'

WIFE EGO	Eyes to the side like I won't notice.
WIFE	'That thing that – '
HUSBAND EGO	eyes to the side – she won't notice.
HUSBAND	'I'm lookin atcha'
WIFE EGO	lookin thru me now like I won't notice that neither
WIFE	'that winds me up – '
HUSBAND	'I'm lookin / atcha – '
WIFE	'that winds me up – you know – you're not – that thing thatcha do – do it on / purpose'
HUSBAND	'I'm lookin – '
WIFE	'do it on purpose to piss me off – '
HUSBAND	'Pissed off are ya? Pissed off are ya?'
WIFE	'Piss me off think you're smart'
HUSBAND	'Just you is it? Pissed off are ya?'
WIFE	'This you fightin?'
HUSBAND	'This ain't fightin.'
WIFE	'This ain't fightin…? This is you "not fightin for it" is it…?
	This is you "not wantin to" is it? This is you not "puttin out" over that prescription is it?
	…Oh.'
HUSBAND	
	Beat.
HUSBAND	'Stand still.'
HUSBAND EGO	She says nuthin then.
WIFE EGO	I got nuthin good to say.

HUSBAND	'Stand still will yer.'
WIFE EGO	Got nuthin good I can be bothered to say.
HUSBAND	'And y'look fine'
HUSBAND EGO	liar
WIFE EGO	he says.
HUSBAND	'Y'look well.'
HUSBAND EGO	Liar.
WIFE EGO	Gives it that.
WIFE	'You stand still.'
WIFE EGO	Think
WIFE	you look better'n I do
WIFE EGO	say
WIFE	'Y'lookin better'n – '
WIFE EGO	lies.
HUSBAND	'No I don't.'
WIFE EGO	
HUSBAND EGO	Clocks me then, then looks away.
WIFE EGO	Hands out the pockets, fraid to be free, fingers on the restless, hands on the shake-down back in again, balled.
WIFE	Show me your hands.
	'Show me your hands – '
HUSBAND	'show me your hands'
WIFE	'you show me yourn first.'
HUSBAND	
HUSBAND	
HUSBAND EGO	This all part a it?
WIFE	'You nervous a me…? Are ya… are yer?'

HUSBAND	
WIFE	
WIFE	'You are ain'tcha.'
HUSBAND	'You ain't what I gotta be nervous of.'
WIFE	'You are ain'tcha, ain'tcha?'
HUSBAND	'What you got I gotta be nervous of?
	What you got – I already got it.'
WIFE	'I already got it.'
HUSBAND	'Got it from you.'
WIFE	'I got it from you.'
HUSBAND	
WIFE	
HUSBAND	'You nervous a that?'
HUSBAND EGO	Eyes on the prescription.
WIFE EGO	Eyes away. Embarrassed.
HUSBAND EGO	Eyes to the floor like there's summat there of interest
WIFE EGO	little on the look away
HUSBAND EGO	she ain't sure where – but away from –
HUSBAND	'What you scared of? What *you* scared of then?'
WIFE	'Not you, for a start.'
HUSBAND	'No?'
WIFE	'No.'
HUSBAND	'… No.
	That?' (*The prescription.*)
WIFE	'No.'
HUSBAND	'No? You sure? You sure? Sure are yer? Are yer?'

| HUSBAND EGO | Cos she doesn't – |
| WIFE EGO | stop shaking. |

Two

'The Child Soldier.'

MUM *and* DAD *are trying to think.*

MUM	Umm.
	Umm…
DAD	Er.
MUM	Umm.
	DAD *coughs.*
	Yes?
DAD	Er…
MUM	Yes?
DAD	Um… you?
MUM	Nothing.
DAD	Nothing?
MUM	…Nothing.
	…I can't think of nothing good…

Three

'The AIDS Genocide. The Prescription.'

HUSBAND

WIFE

WIFE

HUSBAND EGO	Clock it –
WIFE EGO	glance –
HUSBAND EGO	she givin it –
WIFE EGO	glance –
HUSBAND EGO	she givin it, 'fraid to give the prescription the good long look.
WIFE EGO	Eyes to the skies it
HUSBAND EGO	the good long look
WIFE EGO	he eyes to the skies it like how he does –
HUSBAND EGO	the good long look I want to but won't.
WIFE EGO	Like somethin up there's gonna save you.
	WIFE EGO *laughs*.
	Like someone up there's gonna save you.
HUSBAND	
WIFE	
WIFE EGO	Like some higher bein's gonna bother bein here – to save your arse… or mine.
WIFE	'Virgin Mary ain't watchin no more and bet baby Jesus is bored.'
HUSBAND	'What?'
WIFE	'Virgin – '

HUSBAND	'*what*?'
WIFE	'Nuthin.'
HUSBAND	'What?'
WIFE	'It ain't like – '
HUSBAND	'huh?'
WIFE	'It ain't like – it ain't like – '
HUSBAND	'what?'
WIFE EGO	Said
WIFE	'it ain't like I'm becomin critical a your capabilities or somethin – it ain't that, I wouldn't do that. Would I? Husband.'
WIFE EGO	Said.
WIFE	'And I ain't makin a meal over no… manhoodness. Or manhood. Your manhood.'
HUSBAND EGO	What?
WIFE EGO	It ain't that –
HUSBAND EGO	*what*?
WIFE EGO	It ain't that
WIFE	'It ain't that, I wouldn't do that neither. Would I? Would I? Am I?'
WIFE EGO	Said
WIFE	'And I ain't produced the part about providing – '
HUSBAND	'it ain't about that – '
WIFE	'it ain't about that – '
WIFE EGO	said.
WIFE	'It ain't about that, no. Ain't got nuthin to do with the practicalities of what you can provide is it?

…That we can afford one, when what we
need is two…
That we got – one – when what we need
is… two.
That one prescription for life – '

WIFE EGO   for a life

WIFE   'isn't enough for…'

WIFE EGO *shows two fingers*.

'Is it… Now I ain't brought that up.'

WIFE EGO

HUSBAND EGO

WIFE   'Cos I ain't standin here sayin it's me
insteada you – am I?
Ain't here sayin me over you am I?
Not here sayin all the reasons why it
shouldn't be you, am I?
"Should be me. Should be me."
Not sayin that – not doin that.
Am I that? Am I sayin it's that? I
wouldn't bring that up and say that either
would I? Am I sayin that? Like that? No.
I / ain't.'

HUSBAND   'It's not about / that.'

WIFE   'Not about that, no. We're not – '

HUSBAND   'fightin – '

WIFE   'like that – are we. No. No, we're not… '

HUSBAND

WIFE

WIFE   '…But it is you who can't make a course a
meds without messin it up – tabs left in the
bottle – medicine left in the jar – lets one
bout a somethin simple knock you back a
week dunno what to do with yourself.'

HUSBAND	'I liked you lookin after me.'
WIFE`	'You had to be looked after.'
HUSBAND	'You liked lookin after me'
WIFE	'you had to be looked after.'
HUSBAND	'I letchu'
WIFE	'you weren't in no position to not.'
HUSBAND	'In sickness and in health and all / that'
WIFE	'A chill.'
HUSBAND	'A head cold.'
WIFE	'A head cold.'
HUSBAND	'A heavy cold.'
WIFE	'A heavy cold then.'
HUSBAND	'Flu.'
WIFE	'Y'had a chill.
	When have you ever looked after me…?'
HUSBAND	
WIFE	'When have you (ever) – you wouldn't know / how'
HUSBAND	'You're never sick.'
WIFE	'You'd get confused lookin after anyone who weren't you, you would.'
HUSBAND	'You're never / sick – '
WIFE	'You wouldn't know if I was.'
HUSBAND	'You haven't been.'
WIFE	'Till now.'
HUSBAND EGO	Not a shake about her shit now.
HUSBAND	'Thought you was fuckin nervous?'

HUSBAND EGO	Not a shake about / her shit now.
WIFE	'Thought you had somethin to say.'
HUSBAND EGO	Rock solid.
HUSBAND	'Thought you was playin it all that?'
HUSBAND EGO	Not a shake not a tremble –
HUSBAND	'putchur hands on me see how scared I am'
WIFE EGO	no, don't.
HUSBAND EGO	Steady as fuck – mumblin –
WIFE	'no.'
HUSBAND	'What?'
WIFE EGO	Don't.
WIFE	'Like you never heard'
HUSBAND	'like I'm meant to hear'
WIFE	'what.'
HUSBAND	'What?'
WIFE	'No.'
HUSBAND EGO	Won't speak up. She. Won't respond. Me.
HUSBAND	
HUSBAND EGO	Looks away embarrassed. Looks away from it embarrassed – look at her.
HUSBAND	
WIFE	
HUSBAND EGO	Eyes to the floorin it like I've done her somethin.
	Playin powerless
WIFE EGO	play powerless
HUSBAND EGO	playin powerless badly.

WIFE	'What if I wanna look after you?'
HUSBAND	'What if I wanna live lookin after you?
	(I'd) look after you and love it.'
WIFE EGO	Liar.
HUSBAND EGO	Liar.

Somethin down there?
Somethin down there to help her with her sulk?
Helpin her with her shameless?

HUSBAND *runs his fingers through his hair.*

WIFE *watches him.*

WIFE EGO	Usedta be my job. Usually my job, loved me doin it –
WIFE	'love doin it'
HUSBAND	'what?'
WIFE EGO	Fingers thru his follicles... lovely.
HUSBAND EGO	Finish with a fistful of hair. Never used to do this
HUSBAND	'never used to lose this'
WIFE	'what?'
HUSBAND	
WIFE	
HUSBAND EGO	Old.
HUSBAND	
HUSBAND	'Older.'
WIFE EGO	Sad.
WIFE	'Sadder.'
HUSBAND	'What?'

WIFE	'Nuthin.'
HUSBAND EGO	Sick.
WIFE EGO	Sicker.
HUSBAND EGO	Eyes on the lookaway – won't meet mine.
WIFE EGO	Anywhere else – but his.
HUSBAND EGO	Eyes to the skies it like how I do.
WIFE EGO	'Fraid to give it (*Re: the prescription*.) the good long look I want to.
HUSBAND	'We fightin?'
WIFE	
HUSBAND	'Feels like fightin.'
WIFE	'This ain't fightin.'
HUSBAND	'We fightin yet?'
WIFE	'…No.'
HUSBAND	'You finished yet?'
WIFE	'No.'
HUSBAND	'You bored yet?'
WIFE	'…No.'
HUSBAND EGO	Eyes to the skies it like somethin up there's gonna save her like some higher bein would bother bein here
HUSBAND	'God got bored before we did.'
WIFE	'What?'
HUSBAND EGO	Like some higher bein would bother botherin with us.

Four

'The Child Soldier.'

MUM *and* DAD *are trying to think.*

MUM	Umm.
	Umm…
DAD	Er.
MUM	Umm…
	DAD *coughs.*
	Yes?
DAD	Er…
MUM	Yes?
DAD	Um.
MUM	…To watch… to watch him. Lovin that. Lovin doin that. Doing that.

Er.

Hold.
To hold him – his hands his fingers – fingertips, on to him, on to his gaze – into his gaze his any-little-bit-a-him, to hold that – on to that – to have that, into that, to have and to hold that. To have that to hold…

Having that to hold on to.
Having that.
Doing that.
Miss that.

…To smell. Have his smell. Smell his smell, smell his smell on him – smell his smell on me. The never-get-used-to-that, the never-get-enough-of-that – the after-bath aroma, the first thing of a mornin –

the just-come-in-from-out wanting more
of that smell. The smell – lovin that the
smell of lovin that – lovin smellin that.
Me doin that.
Waiting for that.
That smell.
That.
His. Him.
Doin that.
Me.
Miss it.

Umm…

Touch.
Touch him. Doin that –

DAD	said that.
MUM	I said –
DAD	you said that / already
MUM	I said / that?
DAD	You did.
MUM	'To hold,' I said, '*to hold*'
DAD	touch – hold / whatever –
MUM	I'm sayin it again then
DAD	you said – you said – just sayin you said / it already
MUM	to 'touch' him – if that's alright with / *you* –
DAD	nuthin to do with / me –
MUM	nah it never was.
DAD	
MUM	
MUM	To kiss him –

DAD	he hated bein kissed
MUM	by you – to kiss / him
DAD	he hated bein kissed.
MUM	By. You. Hated you trying.
	To kiss him – here… here.
	Catch him off when he weren't watching, land one on him when he weren't ready.

MUM	DAD
Catch him off with a quick – catch him off when I was. Catch him off just because. Catch him with a kiss to comfort.	To watch – to watch him. Watch how he'd watch. Watch how he'd watch back. Watch how he'd watch me back.

DAD   Watch your back while he's watching
               you.
               Watch yourself while he's watching.
               There's that.
               There was that.
               Hold. To hold him. To hold on to him.
               Hold. Touch.
               To hold him down.
               Pin him down.
               Pin him down, play pin him down, play
               down, play hard, play dead. Play till he
               pinned me, till he would pin me – till he
               would pin me to the point of playin for
               real. To the point of playin till there was
               no point – to the point of not playin –
               pinning each other down to prove a point.
               …There's that.
               There's 'playin' that.
               Having to play that.
               There is (that)…

               Beat.

               Umm…

MUM	To smell.
DAD	He smelt of you.
MUM	He smelt of / him –
DAD	he smelt of you.
MUM	He smelt / like –
DAD	He did – he smelt of you – there was no smell of him – there was no smell of him left – he had no smell of his own the only aroma around him was – the only smell left on him was – the only linger left on him was *yourn* – was from *you*.
	The smell of whatever you smothered yourself with – of whatever you drowned yourself in.
	Whatever you drowned yourself in he was drownin right there in the disgustingness of it with yer. The smell of your not-quite-right. The smell of the didn't-cost-much. The smell of the two-for-one. The smell a the been-on-a-bit-too-long –
MUM	you / wouldn't
DAD	the smell a the nuthin-natural-about-it, the nuthin-nice-about-it. He smelt like that –
MUM	you wouldn't / know –
DAD	he smelled like that he smelt like you smell – how you still smell – he smelt of / you.
MUM	You wouldn't know.
DAD	I wouldn't know what he smelt like?
MUM	You wouldn't know what he / smelt like –
DAD	I dunno what anythin smells like.

MUM	You wouldn't know what he smelled like you didn't get close / enough
DAD	I don't know what anythin smells like when you're around
MUM	he wouldn't letchu get close enough to know – you don't get close enough to anything to smell / anything –
DAD	when you're around the smell of anythin else – everything else gets obliterated by your spray-it-as-you-feel-it-full-on artificial / stink.
MUM	You don't get that close and you wouldn't know what he smelled like cos he never letchu get close enough to / him.
DAD	Stinkin out the place – I dunno what you smell like
MUM	I don't want you to smell me.
DAD	You dunno whatchu smell like
MUM	why would I wanna smell myself?
	Why would I wanna smell myself?
DAD	(If) you did you wouldn't / ask –
MUM	Like some kinda dog…
DAD	
MUM	Don't think so. Don't think so – and I don't wantchu near –
DAD	catch the smell a the natural you, drop down dead a / shock.
MUM	Don'tchu come near – don'tchu come nearer –
DAD	genetically modified mothafuckin – you're like that you are, you are – you're like them monster seeds spreadin their monster selves outta their monster labs over the

	happily growin natural shit that was already there, happy growin in the field –
MUM	don'tchu come / nearer
DAD	you're like that you are.
MUM	Stay / there –
DAD	Contaminate – contamination. Contaminate everything you come into contact with, with your / stink –
MUM	I mean it
DAD	genetically modified contaminated fuck contaminating naturally organic me / and he –
MUM	you never got close enough to him to know – you wouldn't know how –
DAD	I wouldn't know / how?
MUM	he never letchu near.

Beat.

DAD	You're never naked of someone else's bottled version of someone else you are – always sprayed up sprayed on – sprayed on ya thick and thorough, spray it on thick and thorough enough might just lose the real you for good – I never get close enough?
MUM	You never get / close enough.
DAD	I never get close enough do I?
MUM	Stay there –
DAD	I never get close –
MUM	don'tchu come – you never wanted to –
DAD	you want me to?
MUM	You never wanted to.

DAD   You want me to? You want me to – you
                             want me close?

MUM

DAD   You want me to now? Do yer? You want
                             me now…?

MUM

DAD

MUM

                             MUM *nods. Just.*

DAD

MUM

MUM

DAD   …Nah. Still don't want you do I?

                             Still don't wanna do yer do I?

                             Beat.

                             His laugh.

MUM

DAD   His laugh.

MUM   …He didn't / laugh.

DAD   His laughter.
                             Me and he's laughter.
                             He laughed with me.

MUM

DAD   Our, more-than-a-smile-or-a-smirk, that
                             we shared –

MUM

DAD   that you never knew nuthin about.

MUM   You don't laugh.

DAD   Our head back, eyes streamin, free, full,
                             frank, full-on – laughter. Laughin hard –

	laughin long – laughin loud like that…
	Over you.
	Having that.
	Doing / that.
MUM	His time.
DAD	Doin / that.
MUM	His time he'd / spend.
DAD	Laughin like that
MUM	his time he'd spend with me –
DAD	laughing at you like that
MUM	the time he'd make to / spend with me
DAD	laughin at your *smell*.
MUM	The time he did spend with me.
DAD	Laughin at y'you and your smell, with me, like that.
	We did.
	That.
	Doin that.
	Miss that.
	Miss that of him.
	I do.
MUM	
MUM	
DAD	
MUM	I wear it cos he bought it.
DAD	He bought it for a joke.
MUM	
DAD	
MUM	I wear it because he liked it.
DAD	He liked it for a joke.
MUM	…It reminds me of / him.

DAD	You are a joke.
	Beat.
MUM	If you were gone –
DAD	I'm not gone tho
MUM	if you were / gone –
DAD	but I'm not the one who's gone / tho.
MUM	if you were gone there'd be nuthin to remind me of you
DAD	I wouldn't wantchu to remember / me
MUM	there's nuthin good to / remember
DAD	I wouldn't want to be remembered.
MUM	Good then.
DAD	Good.
MUM	Good.
DAD	Good.
MUM	*Good.*
	Beat.
DAD	Not by you.

Five

'The Prescription.'

HUSBAND	'I'm not fightin for it'
WIFE EGO	leans back body language denyin his lie.
HUSBAND EGO	She on the front foot for effect.
WIFE	'I'm not gonna act like I won't.'
	Beat.

HUSBAND	'But I am fitter'
WIFE EGO	laid it back like it ent fightin talk
WIFE	'I'm younger.'
HUSBAND	'But I'm stronger.'
HUSBAND EGO	She on the metaphorical lookaway
WIFE	'but I'm smart–'
WIFE EGO	he eyes to the skies it
WIFE	'–ter. I'm smarter. I am.'
HUSBAND	'I earn more – '
WIFE	'not enough to cover two'
HUSBAND	'more'n we need for one.'
WIFE	'What – so the other can watch the other stay well in comfort?'
WIFE EGO	Stung an' on the step back. Nice. Watch – hand out to the side – watch, watch – reachin for the chair –
WIFE	'or enough for a hot hired-in home help?'
HUSBAND EGO	Lean on the chair back
WIFE EGO	think he's gonna fling it –
HUSBAND EGO	she's on the flinch and I don't know why
WIFE EGO	sits instead.
HUSBAND EGO	Sit at her front. Sit at the front of it, sit at her fuckin front of it.
WIFE EGO	He on the lean forward
HUSBAND EGO	she on the step back.
HUSBAND	'You scared a somethin?'
HUSBAND EGO	She eyes away it.
WIFE EGO	Doin the dance that we do.

WIFE	'What I gotta be scared of?'
HUSBAND	It's me who's scared a you
WIFE	what?
WIFE EGO	Mumblin – mumblin –
WIFE	'what?'
HUSBAND	It's me who's –
WIFE	'what?'
HUSBAND	'It's me who's scared a you.'
WIFE EGO	He on the lean back.
HUSBAND EGO	She eases forward.
HUSBAND	'I can earn more.'
WIFE	'I can adapt more.'
HUSBAND	'I can work longer – '
WIFE	'I can work nearer.'
WIFE EGO	Eyes to the floor. Eyes to the sky then. He eyes the gods and away from anywhere near me.
WIFE	'Lookin for somethin?'
WIFE EGO	He eyes to the skies stayin / there.
WIFE	'Lookin for something?'
HUSBAND	'I can support the girls – '
WIFE	'this ain't about the girls'
HUSBAND	'I can / support – '
WIFE	'you bringin the girls into this? Don't be bringing our girls / into this.'
HUSBAND	'I can talk to the girls'
WIFE	'our girls don't need talkin to – '
HUSBAND	'I can support / the girls'

H. AND WIFE EGO	fight.
WIFE	'I can raise the girls – '
H. AND WIFE EGO	fight.
HUSBAND	'I can teach the girls'
H. AND WIFE EGO	fight
WIFE	'what?'
HUSBAND	'I can teach the girls – '
WIFE	'exactly *what*?'
H. AND WIFE EGO	*Fight* –
WIFE	'Firstborn don't need teachin and Mary thinks she knows it all.'
HUSBAND	'Where she get that from?'
WIFE	'I wonder.'
HUSBAND	'Do that.'
HUSBAND EGO	Mouth on her like her mother.
HUSBAND	'Mary's like her mother – '
WIFE	'an' Firstborn's like her father – God help / her – '
HUSBAND	'They'll need their father.'
HUSBAND EGO	Me.
WIFE EGO	Fight.
WIFE	'The *girls'll* need their *mother*.'
WIFE EGO	Me.
HUSBAND EGO	Fight.
HUSBAND	'I can protect the girls – '
WIFE	'*I* can protect the / girls – '
HUSBAND	'you don't call this fightin?'
WIFE	'This ain't fightin – '

HUSBAND	'you wouldn't call this / fightin?'
WIFE	'This ain't fightin – '
HUSBAND	'This ain't fightin?'
WIFE	'This ain't fightin – you still standin an' the prescription ain't mine / yet'
HUSBAND	'I'm not gonna make like to fight you / for it – '
WIFE	'I'm not gonna act like I – '

The CHILD SOLDIER *stands with them, with his bloodied machete.*

His head is shaved down to a number one.

HUSBAND *and* WIFE *are both taken by surprise.*

Six

'The Child Soldier.'

DAD	Outta things to say? You run outta good things to say?
	You run outta things to say / about him?
MUM	There's not enough words –
DAD	that you know –
MUM	there's not enough good words –
DAD	that you know –
MUM	not enough good long words out there to say about him – about my son
DAD	*my son*
MUM	not enough of them – so I'll stop.

DAD	Wish you would.
MUM	I'll say nuthin.
DAD	Wish you would.
MUM	There is nothing to say –
DAD	there's plenty to say – there was plenty / to say –
MUM	don't start
DAD	before you –
MUM	don't / start
DAD	lost him –
MUM	*don't*. His hair – his hair – .
DAD	
MUM	His hair. Lovin that. His (hair) – his cut of his hair –
DAD	he had my hair
MUM	he did not
DAD	had my hair / line
MUM	he did not.
DAD	He got his hair from / me
MUM	he did *not*. His cut of how he'd wear his hair… Letting me cut his hair – doing that. Seeing that. Fingers thru that. To see that. Have that. Have that remind me – have that remind me of –
DAD	mine.
MUM	How yourn weren't.
	How yourn weren't ever quite – able – weren't never quite… was it? Of how

	yourn usedta be – how yourn usedta *try* to be – when you used to *try* to bother –
DAD	when there was something worth bothering about
MUM	even then you never got it right – get it right
DAD	when you were worth bothering about
MUM	still weren't worth waitin / for –
DAD	before I realised there was no point. It was / pointless.
MUM	You still weren't worth waitin for even then, still / weren't worth that
DAD	it was pointless. You were / pointless.
MUM	and even when you tried – what you called 'tried' – what / you passed for 'tried' –
DAD	you are pointless and it was pointless / trying
MUM	even that hadda knack a not lookin right. Never looked right. Always somethin not-right-lookin about yer.
	Beat.
DAD	You weren't worth trying over – y'weren't worth workin that hard over… Didn't have to work that hard to work you over – Did I?
MUM	
DAD	
MUM	His hair looked better'n yourn ever would –
DAD	in fact you was easy –
MUM	better'n yourn ever / could

DAD	very easy.
MUM	You weren't able.
DAD	Bit of a bike.
MUM	Outshone by our son.
DAD	Somethin of the slag about yer.
MUM	Every time.
DAD	Somethin of the slut –
MUM	*all* the time
DAD	somethin of the *used* about yer.
	Beat.
MUM	To watch –
DAD	you'd watch –
MUM	you'd watch –
DAD	I never.
MUM	You would –
DAD	I never –
MUM	yes you did – you'd watch him – you'd watch him – you watched you did. Watch his hair and wish it was you – watch me wash it and wish it was you –
DAD	I never –
MUM	watch me cuttin it, wishin it was / you –
DAD	I never / lost
MUM	you watched you watched you did – I watched you watchin, I saw yer – pathetic
DAD	I never – (lost him.)
MUM	pitiful.
DAD	I never lost him –

MUM	pitiful. You are –
DAD	did I?
MUM	Pitiful and pathetic hand in hand you / are –
DAD	He weren't with me.
MUM	He was never with you –
DAD	he weren't out with me –
MUM	you never took him out –
DAD	he loved our inside time –
MUM	he loved goin out with me more –
DAD	till you lost him.
MUM	They *took* –
DAD	till you / lost –
MUM	I never lost him – I didn't I didn't I didn't… They took him. They took him. They *took* him.
	They did.
DAD	
MUM	
MUM	
MUM	
DAD	Wash it now…
MUM	
DAD	Run your hands over his number one now.
MUM	
DAD	Put your hands to his head now.
MUM	
DAD	And see where it gets you.

Seven

'The Child Soldier.'

HUSBAND *and* WIFE *(from 'The Prescription').*

The CHILD SOLDIER *still holds his machete.*

HUSBAND	There's nuthin –
WIFE	there is / nuthin –
HUSBAND	there is nothing –
WIFE	we don't have –
HUSBAND	nothing – we don't / got –
WIFE	if he's lookin for / somethin
HUSBAND	we don't –
WIFE	have it.
HUSBAND	If you're lookin for somethin –
WIFE	if he's lookin for / somethin –
HUSBAND	y'wanna look somewhere else go somewhere / else
WIFE	somewhere / else
HUSBAND	anywhere else
WIFE	for your somethin.
HUSBAND	Cos we've got nuthin here.
WIFE	We don't
HUSBAND	we don't
WIFE	we don't –
HUSBAND	have anything –
WIFE	we / don't –

HUSBAND	for yer. Something ain't here, nuthin ain't here – if somethin was here we'd say if anything was here we'd tell yer –
WIFE	honest.
HUSBAND	Honest – there's –
WIFE	there is / nuthin
HUSBAND	there is nothing –
WIFE	we don't / have
HUSBAND	nuthin here –
WIFE	no. No.
HUSBAND	Anything here.
WIFE	No. No.
HUSBAND	Something here for yer. Honest…
	Honest.
HUSBAND	
CHILD	
WIFE	
CHILD	
HUSBAND	
WIFE	
WIFE	Except – if it's food –
HUSBAND	do you want food?
WIFE	Does he want / food?
HUSBAND	This isn't –
WIFE	is it / food?
HUSBAND	about that.
WIFE	We have that we have that we have that if that's what you want – if that's the

	somethin you want we have that but apart from / that –
HUSBAND	Apart / from –
WIFE	apart from that
HUSBAND	we don't have nuthin.
WIFE	There is –
HUSBAND	nuthin –
WIFE	there / is
HUSBAND	there is nothin – there is nothin here for you – that we have...
WIFE	No.
	Except food...
HUSBAND	Apart from that –
WIFE	apart from that – no there is –
HUSBAND	nuthin else.
WIFE	No. No.
CHILD	
HUSBAND	
CHILD	
HUSBAND	
WIFE	Except – if it's money
HUSBAND	if you came for money
WIFE	is it money?
HUSBAND	If you came / for that
WIFE	Does he want / money?
HUSBAND	Is this about that?
WIFE	If he needs –
HUSBAND	you want –

WIFE	does he need –
HUSBAND	look d'you / want –
WIFE	some money?
HUSBAND	We don't –
WIFE	is it that?
HUSBAND	We don't / have –
WIFE	Is it that?
HUSBAND	We don't got / any –
WIFE	A bit.
HUSBAND	We don't have –
WIFE	only a bit
HUSBAND	any money. We don't.
WIFE	…Just a bit.

WIFE digs into HUSBAND's front trouser pockets and pulls out his coins. She shows to the CHILD SOLDIER. He doesn't respond.

…Apart from / that…

HUSBAND	Apart from –
WIFE	apart from that –
HUSBAND	there's nothing…

There's nothing that we have for you.

WIFE   No. No.

There is nothing for you here – tell him. Tell him. Tell him that.

Beat.

CHILD

WIFE

WIFE	Except my ring.
HUSBAND	…This isn't about –
WIFE	my rings
HUSBAND	it's not about –
WIFE	both my rings
HUSBAND	it's not about that.
	Is it?
WIFE	They come off –
HUSBAND	this is / about
WIFE	I can gettem off –
HUSBAND	this is about somethin –
WIFE	I can get them / off.
HUSBAND	this is about something else.
WIFE	I can I can. I can. If that's what you / want.
HUSBAND	He doesn't / want –
WIFE	if that's what he's here / for –
HUSBAND	he's not here for that
WIFE	If that's what he needs…
	WIFE *continually tries to twist her rings off. They won't come.*
	Apart from this –
HUSBAND	this / is –
WIFE	apart from them
HUSBAND	this is / about
WIFE	after that
HUSBAND	this is about us.

WIFE	We have nothing else –
HUSBAND	this is about us.
WIFE	…Will he go?
HUSBAND	Isn't it?

Beat.

Us not being them.

Cos we're not them.

Cos there is nuthin / else.

WIFE	No. No. *Tell him*…
HUSBAND	And he's not here for / the –
WIFE	It's not much.
HUSBAND	And he's not come for / the –
WIFE	I know it's not / much –
HUSBAND	he's not here for that
WIFE	but this'll be everything.
HUSBAND	There's nothing
WIFE	there is / nothing
HUSBAND	yes there's nothing –
WIFE	no.
HUSBAND	There is nothing – there's nothing – there is nothing else –
WIFE	no. No.
HUSBAND	There is nothing else we can do…

Is there. Is there? Is there.

CHILD	
HUSBAND	
CHILD	

HUSBAND

>WIFE *offers up the prescription to the* CHILD SOLDIER.
>
>*Beat.*
>
>*The* CHILD SOLDIER *destroys it.*

CHILD   Beg.

Eight

'Stoning Mary.'

YOUNGER SISTER (MARY) *wears heavy glasses.*

CORR. OFFICER   …Mary.

OLDER SISTER

YOUNGER SISTER

OLDER SISTER

OLDER SISTER

OLDER SISTER   Since when you gotta thing with your things?

>Since when you gotta thing with your things?

YOUNGER SISTER Huh?

OLDER SISTER   How long since you –

YOUNGER SISTER I dunno

OLDER SISTER   since when didju – ?

YOUNGER SISTER I dunno.

OLDER SISTER   You dunno? You dunno? Y'don't know?

>*Beat.*

...Stressful...

Don't suit yer do they –

YOUNGER SISTER I / dunno

OLDER SISTER dunno much do yer they don't even suit – they don't – you need 'em?

YOUNGER SISTER I –

OLDER SISTER Still gotcha hair then. Letchu still got that?

YOUNGER SISTER

OLDER SISTER S'grown.

YOUNGER SISTER

OLDER SISTER Make you look older – make you look old – make you look – they do – they don't – someone said they did – whoever said they did was lyin – who in here said that then, four eyes?

YOUNGER SISTER

OLDER SISTER Huh? Huh?

YOUNGER SISTER No one.

OLDER SISTER They was lyin – make y'look – they do, make y'look... not like you – not like you look – not like how you look.
Usedta.
Usedta look.
Before.
Looked before.
Before you haddem you seen yourself, Sis?

YOUNGER SISTER

OLDER SISTER You seen yourself – you seen yourself in em?

YOUNGER SISTER ...Yeh –

OLDER SISTER   no you ain't.
Someone say they look nice…?
Someone say they look alright – yeh?

YOUNGER SISTER No

OLDER SISTER   cos they ain't.

Someone say they look the shit? They
was lyin – cos they don't – you think
they look alright?

You think they look alright?

YOUNGER SISTER

OLDER SISTER   You think they look alright?

YOUNGER SISTER I –

OLDER SISTER   you don't know – you wouldn't know
you wouldn't know you never did know –
cos they don't – they don't – they don't
suit they don't even suit yer and how
long you had a thing with your things
then?

YOUNGER SISTER I / dunno.

OLDER SISTER   Don' look good at all do they. Do they.
Do they?

Do they?

Beat.

Nah. No. They do not.

You goin blind – sight shot to shit is / it?

YOUNGER SISTER No.

OLDER SISTER   Not no fuckin fashion accessory tho are
they – are they?

Are they?

YOUNGER SISTER

OLDER SISTER   Don't think so… No.

                  Beat.

YOUNGER SISTER No.

OLDER SISTER   No. They ain't – you get tested – you
                  long or short?

YOUNGER SISTER They said –

OLDER SISTER   love someone to test my shit – check my
                  shit – check me out – get me tested –

YOUNGER SISTER they think / I'm –

OLDER SISTER   love to – love that. Love to love that. But
                  no. No chance. Me have that? – I don't
                  think so. Me have somethin? – I don't
                  think so. Someone give a fuck – so very
                  fuckin no. You requess a test or did they
                  offer – bet they was on the offer – little
                  freeness for yer – you goin blind or
                  somethin – look how thick they are – how
                  thick are they? How thick is them things?

YOUNGER SISTER I ent goin / blind.

OLDER SISTER   *Thick* thick. I could be an' no one would
                  care no one would give a fuck – I could
                  be goin blind and no one wouldn't know
                  – no one wouldn't wanna know – know
                  to not give a fuck know to do that – know
                  how to do that – easy – an' they look like
                  bottle ends look like vases look like they
                  gone and got a bit happy on the thickness
                  front – had a ton a glass left over and
                  stuck 'em on the front a your face – they
                  look fuckin 'orrible.
                  Look like you got a problem –
                  look like you a bit back-a-the-class –
                  bit on the 'don't knows' –
                  bit on the retardative, you long or short of
                  it or what – which is the what / of it?

YOUNGER SISTER   When things is / close –

OLDER SISTER   Mine could be worse – worse'n yourn –
you lucky.

You know, y'know? You're lucky to
know – I'm here without a whatever
thinkin my what I'm seein is normal
when it might not ain't – when it might
be fallin well short of what it should be –
when I might be more'n half than blind
meself and worse'n yourn ever is.

Beat.

Least you know... at least you know...
y'know?... Love someone to test my
shit... would love that...

YOUNGER SISTER   They asked –

OLDER SISTER   see –

YOUNGER SISTER   offered –

OLDER SISTER   bet they did –

YOUNGER SISTER   they –

OLDER SISTER *shakes out two
cigarettes.*

OLDER SISTER   see – what, what – and what? So's yous
can see what you're doin better – see
yourself doin nuthin in here better'n you
did before – see what they're doin to you
better'n that – you can see what they
gonna do better still – and you ain't one
to refuse you ain't one to knock back a
bit a freeness is it – is it – what – what?

No you ent – what?... What? You
stopped?

YOUNGER SISTER   I've –

OLDER SISTER   you on the health kick?

YOUNGER SISTER I've stopped.

OLDER SISTER You who the one who got me started. You the one who started me down that road is gonna sit there and say to me you stopped – nah – I know you ain't – I know you ain't… I know you *ain't* – I know you ain't gonna sit there and gimme *that*.

Beat.

…Since when?

YOUNGER SISTER I / dunno.

OLDER SISTER Since before or after you started sportin your additional eyewear – this the new you – this the new (you) – you goin out healthier'n you was ever in – you plannin on doin that and how much things we do?

YOUNGER SISTER I / dunno –

OLDER SISTER How much things we do together?

YOUNGER SISTER I / dunno.

OLDER SISTER How much things we – can we – do we got left to do?

YOUNGER SISTER

OLDER SISTER Yeh. No. You don't know. People that I put on hold – you don't know – dealins to do that I didn't – y'don't (know) – cos I'm dealin with you cos I'm doin that makin that choice – makin *a* choice – which is whatchu want – you don't know 'bout that do yer?

No you do not.

Me, don't say nuthin cos I don't wantchu knowin – don't want the 'ohh iss alright' – don't wantchur 'sorries' – don't wantchu feelin guiltier'n you already are.

Don't clock that do yer?

Don't think about that?
Do yer. Do yer. Do yer?
...No you do not.

Come in here – what – what? Wanta little
spark-up you sayin you've stopped.
Come in here – what – when I coulda
sparked up out there and you in here say
you've stopped.
Come in here to share the thing we usedta
do and now you sayin you don't cos you
on some health-kick or some such shit –
you ain't stopped – you ain't stopped.
You ent stopped... have yer?

No you have (not) – I coulda.
I coulda.
I coulda I coulda stopped couldn't I?

YOUNGER SISTER   Couldja.

OLDER SISTER   I coulda stopped coulda stopped if I
hadn't started coulda stopped if I hadn't
got started – someone hadn't *got* me
started in the first fuckin place *Sis* –
couldn't I? Couldn't I?

Beat.

Thank you.

...So you ain't in no position to quit. You
don't get the say-so to say you've
stopped. You don't got the right – you
lost the right – you lost that right when
you started me startin – you lost the right
before you lost your rights, right?

Yeh you did –

YOUNGER SISTER   I didn't haveta come thru.

OLDER SISTER   *I* didn't haveta come.

I didn't haveta come.
I didn't have to come did I? Did I. *Did I?*
– No I did not – and I'm fine thanks –
I'm fuckin fine – I'm doin alright –
thanks. Thanks for askin.
I'm bearin up – y'know. Y'know. You
know?
Not.

YOUNGER SISTER

OLDER SISTER   Huh?

YOUNGER SISTER

OLDER SISTER   *Yeh. Stressful.*

YOUNGER SISTER   I –

OLDER SISTER   yeh. It is.

        Beat.

YOUNGER SISTER   …Sorry.

OLDER SISTER   Not enough.
        Not good enough.
        Not accepted Mary.
        Not now. Not ever.

        OLDER SISTER *sparks up her cigarette
        alone and smokes.*

        Pause.

YOUNGER SISTER   …How many people signed my
        petition…?

Nine

'The Child Soldier.'

The CHILD SOLDIER *sits next to his* (*the*) MUM *and* DAD, *passive*.

MUM

MUM

MUM

DAD

MUM	His voice.
	His voice –
DAD	What?
MUM	His voice –
DAD	there's nuthin nice about his / voice.
MUM	his voice –
DAD	there's nuthin nice about his voice – if we're bein honest –
MUM	his tone and his… his softness and his… and how he'd call me and / use his…
DAD	There is nuthin nice about it – there is nuthin nice left about it.
MUM	His / voice –
DAD	His shoutin or his screamin voice?
MUM	His –
DAD	if we're bein honest – his screamin or his threatening voice?
MUM	As you're pinning him down or have you let him up by now?
DAD	His lyin voice or his cryin / voice?

MUM   How he speaks to me is different to how
                   he speaks to you.

DAD   He doesn't speak.

MUM   To you.

DAD   He doesn't / speak

MUM   To you

DAD   he / doesn't.

MUM   how you speak to me –

DAD   he doesn't / speak

MUM   is disgraceful – he doesn't speak to me
                   how you speak to me – how you speak to
                   me is different to how I speak to you and
                   how he speaks to me is different from
                   that – we talk –

DAD   you don't talk.

MUM   We can talk.

DAD   Butchu don't.

MUM   I speak what I gotta / say –

DAD   I speak what I gotta say

MUM   you spit what you gotta say / back –

DAD   he doesn't speak he barks

MUM   to you.

DAD   He barks his demands and shouts his
                   curses –

MUM   to you. He speaks to me

DAD   he shouts at you

MUM   at you

DAD   at you first

MUM   at you for bein you

DAD	at you for bein you and stinkin a that cheap shit still and still bein here when he weren't and losin him in the first fuckin / place –
MUM	I never lost (him) – they took –
DAD	*I* never lost him – screams at you for / that
MUM	and cursin me now are ya? Cursin at me now are ya?
DAD	I –
MUM	effin and blindin at me now are yer?
DAD	I'm sayin –
MUM	me or him is it this time? Which?
DAD	I'm just sayin –
MUM	me or him is it this time – which – cos I can't tell and it weren't / my –
DAD	you can spit your venom back –
MUM	it weren't my fault they took –
DAD	all you want –
MUM	they *took* him –
DAD	all you want, cos I sleep at night.
MUM	…Sit there sayin your shit
DAD	I can sleep at night – if we're bein / honest –
MUM	all your shit – in your shit – grunting in the corner.
DAD	When did you last have the full eight hours a the beauty / sleep?
MUM	I don't need / no –
DAD	Yeh you do –

MUM	I don't need no sleep – sleep ent what I / want
DAD	y'need somethin –
MUM	sleep ent what I / need
DAD	y'need somethin –
MUM	I don't sleep
DAD	see.
MUM	I can't sleep
DAD	see.
MUM	…If we're bein honest… I can't sleep. If we are bein that – if we're being that – are we being that?

Beat.

I can't sleep with him in the house…
I can't sleep with him back in the house.

Beat.

He scares me.

Ten

'Stoning Mary.'

OLDER SIST____   ____y.
          ____y 'n' strong.
          ____nat'd (*Gasps*.) me.
     B____ ____f it.
Crates a it.

No glass necessary suck it straight from
source, bottle up head back – lash it
down. Lovely. Lace me down like that.

...Somethin to the side... with somethin good cooked to the side. Something home-cooked to the side to go with and if I was you – if you was me and I was you – which we obviously ain't – but if we was – and I wouldn't be in here where you are if we did was that, but if we was – an' how good would that be for you havin a taste a how it is to be me, how fuckin good it is to be me –

not

if I was you – I'd be well glad I weren't me – but would be askin you for somethin home cooked to go with.

Taste a my walk thru – thru what I go thru cos a you...

If I was you I'd look at me and think 'shit' – look at me and think 'fuckin hell' – look at me and thank fuck I weren't me goin thru what I go thru cos a *you* – have the bottle to give thanks to the church a 'fuckall' an' all over the that's-how-it-is. If I was.
And if you was me and I was you...

Wouldn't be wearin them friggin things in fronta my face for a start – prefer to look sweet and squint, I would – I would –

YOUNGER SISTER   If I was / you –

OLDER SISTER   if I was *you* – somethin home-cooked to go with – if I was you I'd make you do that cos you could cook, you could cook, you always could cook – give you that – couldn't yer?
Call you you'd do me a dish a somethin on the homemade hot an' spectacular – on the hypothetical that we're talkin – somethin fancy to go with the crate a

fizzy that'd be feelin its way to fuckin me
up – thass what I'd do.

Thass what I'd do.
Thass what I'd want.
That's what I'd ask for – if I / was you.

YOUNGER SISTER If you was me and I was you I wouldn't
cook it.

Beat.

OLDER SISTER …Yeh you would.

YOUNGER SISTER …I wouldn't.

OLDER SISTER You would –

YOUNGER SISTER I / wouldn't.

OLDER SISTER you would you would you would –

YOUNGER SISTER I wouldn't.

OLDER SISTER I'd make yer.

YOUNGER SISTER I –

OLDER SISTER I'd make yer I'd make yer. Wouldn't I.
Wouldn't I?

OLDER SISTER

OLDER SISTER

YOUNGER SISTER

YOUNGER SISTER …What if I never got your when-you-
rangs to say what cookin up you
wanted…

Never picked up. Never answered. Swear
down I never got the message. Swear
down more the VO never come…
Said I was out when I weren't…
Said I was away when I weren't…
Said I never got it when / I did…

OLDER SISTER You tryinta be funny?

YOUNGER SISTER   If I was that – you bein me, me bein you
– I couldn't cook yer nuthin if I never
heard nuthin from yer for years you'd
haveta think a somethin else then, haveta
think a someone else then...
Hypothetically speakin.

OLDER SISTER   See I – 'me-as-you' woulda allocated my
once a week to someone who would take
it. To someone who would wannit, as I'm
sure you – 'you-as-me' – would have told
your – 'me you' – from time. And if I
was you, I woulda clocked it and dialled
somewhere else.
Cos – 'you me' – mighta got sick and
tired a takin reverse charged allocated
anything from 'me you' – that 'you me'
didn't want – didn't ask for, and could
well do without.
Hypothetically friggin / speakin.

YOUNGER SISTER   What if your – 'you me' – never had no
one else to call?

OLDER SISTER   I'd ask my 'me you' self why. If I was
still *you*.
Which I wouldn't be...
Which I couldn't be.
Could I. Could I? Could I?
Andju wouldn't be my allocated call
anyway.

YOUNGER SISTER   I wouldn't pick up.

OLDER SISTER   I know.

YOUNGER SISTER   I wouldn't be in.

OLDER SISTER   I know.

YOUNGER SISTER   I wouldn't come.

OLDER SISTER   See you juss answered your own next
question then so don't bother askin why
I didn't.

And twelve.

YOUNGER SISTER

YOUNGER SISTER   Twelve?

OLDER SISTER   Twelve people signed.

YOUNGER SISTER

OLDER SISTER   Put their pen to your petition. Twelve.

YOUNGER SISTER   Twelve's after ten, right?

OLDER SISTER   After eleven

YOUNGER SISTER   which is after ten, right?

OLDER SISTER

YOUNGER SISTER   How many did I need?

OLDER SISTER   Six thousand.

YOUNGER SISTER

YOUNGER SISTER

Pause.

OLDER SISTER   S'after a lotta tens / Mary.

YOUNGER SISTER   I know.

YOUNGER SISTER

YOUNGER SISTER

OLDER SISTER   Somethin fuckin fizzy to slowly fuck me up is what I'd ask for as my lass requess – thass my requess, would be my last request… if I was you.

Which I'm not.

So what is it you said to them you want as yourn?

Beat.

YOUNGER SISTER   You. To come.

Eleven

'The Child Soldier.'

MUM, SON (CHILD SOLDIER) *and* DAD.

Pause. Silence.

The SON *sniffs.*

DAD *smirks.*

The SON *sniffs again.*

SON *raises the game and sniffs more obviously.*

MUM *shifts. Uncomfortable.*

DAD *watches her, amused.*

DAD	You alright?... Love.
MUM	
	SON sniffs.
	DAD enjoys MUM's discomfort.
MUM	
DAD	Are you?
	SON laughs a little.
MUM	I'm...
	Is he...?
DAD	Why, I don't know. Is he?
MUM	...Is he alright?
DAD	...Are you alright?
SON	
DAD	He's 'fine'.
MUM	Is he?
DAD	Are yer?

MUM	He's not.
DAD	Are yer?
SON	Tell her to ask me.
MUM	
DAD	Ask him.
MUM	
SON	
DAD	
DAD	Ask him.
SON	Tell her to ask me
DAD	he says for you to…
MUM	
DAD	She says she –
SON	tell her to ask me.
DAD	He says for / you to –
MUM	Tell him I can't.
SON	Tell her she will.

Beat.

DAD   …Why don't you ask him aye…?

Just ask him how he is.

SON *sniffs*.

Ask him. Ask. Go on.

MUM	
MUM	
SON	

Beat.

MUM   …How… are…

How are…

…What-did-you-do…?

Pause.

SON   Tell her I am.

DAD   He says he –

SON   tell her I'm *fine*.

MUM

SON

SON   …Tell her she smells nice.

DAD

DAD

DAD   …He said… he said / you…

SON   Tell her.

DAD   …He said –

SON   *say it.*

MUM   Do I?

SON *smirks.*

Oh.

Twelve

'Stoning Mary.'

OLDER SISTER   What'll happen to them – what'll happen to them then?

YOUNGER SISTER   No one I know is gonna be there.

OLDER SISTER   What'll happen to them then? You gonna / wear them?

YOUNGER SISTER   You gonna / come?

OLDER SISTER   You gonna go out with them on – gonna
                      go out there with them on you gonna go
                      out lookin / like that?

YOUNGER SISTER   You comin?

OLDER SISTER   Picture in the paper – picture in the paper
                      of you, of you out there – out there with /
                      them on –

YOUNGER SISTER   They'll shave my head.

OLDER SISTER   I'd taken 'em off

YOUNGER SISTER   then strip me down

OLDER SISTER   I'd take 'em right off toldja

YOUNGER SISTER   then lead me out

OLDER SISTER   take 'em off – give 'em to charity

YOUNGER SISTER   are you gonna come?

OLDER SISTER   Give 'em to charity –

YOUNGER SISTER   cos they're expectin crowds

OLDER SISTER   – like some charity would want 'em.

YOUNGER SISTER   They're expectin crowds.
                      They're expectin a good crowd.
                      If they get good weather.
                      Get good weather they get good numbers.
                      So if you're comin. You gonna needta
                      book – if you're comin. Cos they gonna
                      charge.
                      But I can getchu a comp…
                      Cos you family.
                      They're expectin… (a good crowd)… if
                      it don't rain.
                      They're expectin… women's groups
                      block-booking almost booked it out – the
                      same bitches that wouldn't back me, the
                      same womens that wouldn't sign – them
                      same womens is block-bookin it out.
                      How many people marched for me?

OLDER SISTER

YOUNGER SISTER   More'n who signed for me?

OLDER SISTER

YOUNGER SISTER   ...Anybody march for me? How many
did that?

Less than ten?

OLDER SISTER   You spectin some stay of exe-somethin?

YOUNGER SISTER   Got no stay of exe-fuckin-nuthin have I.

...Not even the women. Not even the
women?

OLDER SISTER   ...No.

YOUNGER SISTER   So what happened to the womanist
bitches?
...The feminist bitches?
...The professional bitches.
What happened to them?

What about the burn-their-bra bitches?
The black bitches
the rootsical bitches
the white the brown bitches
the right-on bitches
what about *them*?

What happened to the mainstream
bitches?
The rebel bitches
the underground bitches
what about – how 'bout –
the bitches that support other bitches?

Bitches that ain't but got nuthin better to do
bitches that gotta conscience
underclass bitches
overclass bitches
political bitches – what about – how
'bout –
what happened to *them*?

The bitches that love to march?
The bitches that love to study
the music-lovin bitches
the shebeen queen bitches
the bitches that love to fight
the bitches that love a debate
the bitches that love to curse?
The lyrical bitches
the educated bitches
the full-uppa-attitude bitches
the high-upsed rich-list lady bitch –
bitches
whadafuckabout them?

The bitches that love their men
the bitches that love other bitches' men
the bitches that juss love bitches –
what about alla them then?

…Not one a them would march for me?

OLDER SISTER

YOUNGER SISTER   Not a one a them would sign for me?

OLDER SISTER   …Well… twelve did.

YOUNGER SISTER   Where's all the bitches that'll support a
bitch, huh?
Out there supportin other bitches –
bitches that ain't me.
Where's all the bitches that'll protest a
bitch, eh?
Protestin for other bitches – bitches that
ain't me.
Bitches that can read.
Bitches that can count.
Pretty bitches.
Easy-on-the-eye bitches I betcha –

OLDER SISTER   butchu –

YOUNGER SISTER   but I'ma bitch in need

OLDER SISTER   butchu killed / a –

YOUNGER SISTER   I got cause

OLDER SISTER   you killed a man.

YOUNGER SISTER

YOUNGER SISTER   And I'm gonna be stoned down for it.

OLDER SISTER

YOUNGER SISTER

OLDER SISTER   You killed a man who was a boy.

YOUNGER SISTER   …That *boy* was a soldier.

Beat.

OLDER SISTER   That soldier was a child –

YOUNGER SISTER   that *child* killed my parents.
Our parents, *ourn*.
…I done somethin.
Least I done somethin. I done somethin –
I did. I did. I did – I done somethin.

YOUNGER SISTER

OLDER SISTER

YOUNGER SISTER   Mum and Dad'd be – they would.

Would've.

They'da been prouda / me.

OLDER SISTER   If they was here.

YOUNGER SISTER   And they woulda been if he hadn't done
what he did – ourn weren't his first, he'd
killed other people – ourn weren't his
first was they?

Was they? Sis?

OLDER SISTER   If they was here. They wouldn't come.
Mum and Dad wouldn'ta come.

YOUNGER SISTER   I wouldn't be in here for them to come to.

OLDER SISTER   You wouldn't be in here for them to not come to.
They wouldn'ta come.
They couldn'ta come.

YOUNGER SISTER They would.

OLDER SISTER   They couldn't.

YOUNGER SISTER They would.

OLDER SISTER   They couldn't.

YOUNGER SISTER They would –

OLDER SISTER   they couldn't – not by now.

YOUNGER SISTER What?

What?

OLDER SISTER

YOUNGER SISTER

YOUNGER SISTER What?

OLDER SISTER   Nuthin –

YOUNGER SISTER what?

OLDER SISTER

YOUNGER SISTER 'Nuthin'?

OLDER SISTER   Nuthin… No… Sis. 'Nuthin.'

OLDER SISTER

YOUNGER SISTER

Beat.

Betcha bitches'll come to my stonin, betchu they do.

Betcha bitches'll come out for that tho.
Bring a bitch fuckin picnic and make the effort.

Dressed like a bitch on occasion as they
watch.
Bet iss a bitch be first in the queue...

Be first to fuckin throw...

Fuck it.
Fuck 'em.
Fuck them.
You gonna come – are you gonna come?

OLDER SISTER   I –

YOUNGER SISTER you comin then? Comin then? You comin
then – are yer?

OLDER SISTER

YOUNGER SISTER You gonna come then? Are yer – are yer
are yer ?

OLDER SISTER

YOUNGER SISTER You are – you'll come you'll come you'll
come won'tcha – won't yer – wont yer?
You will – you will you will. Promise
me. Promise me you'll come.

OLDER SISTER   ...Are you gonna wear them?

YOUNGER SISTER

OLDER SISTER

            OLDER SISTER *nods*.

YOUNGER SISTER

OLDER SISTER

YOUNGER SISTER ...Fuckin... twelve.

Thirteen

'The Child Soldier.'

MUM *is trying to cry.*

DAD

DAD

DAD

DAD   Ain't workin is it.

                 Ain't fallin is it. Are they?
                 Are they? Are they?

                 She did you your fuckin favour...

                 I know how dry your eyes were when he
                 was with us – and I can see how dry your
                 eyes are. Even now.

Fourteen

'The Prescription.'

O. SISTER EGO

BOYFRIEND EGO

OLDER SISTER

BOYFRIEND

BOYFRIEND   'We fightin?'

OLDER SISTER   'No.'

BOYFRIEND   'I ain't fightin.'

O. SISTER EGO   I said

OLDER SISTER   'You fightin me?'

BOYFRIEND EGO   Tell her –

BOYFRIEND	'No.'
O. SISTER EGO	(I) said
OLDER SISTER	'You're fightin me for it.'
BOYFRIEND	'I ain't fightin.'
O. SISTER EGO	Go on.
BOYFRIEND EGO	Go on.
O. SISTER EGO	He is.
BOYFRIEND EGO	She is.
OLDER SISTER	'You're fightin me for it. You are you are. You are tho – an' stand still – '
BOYFRIEND	'(You) come a bit closer (you) know that I can't – '
O. SISTER EGO	don't
OLDER SISTER	'can if you wanted to – '
BOYFRIEND EGO	again
BOYFRIEND	'(you) come a bit closer (you) know that I can't stand / still – '
O. SISTER EGO	no
OLDER SISTER	'nuthin but – '
O. SISTER EGO	nerves
BOYFRIEND	'what? 'Nuthin but' what? You put your hands on me you'd know.'
BOYFRIEND EGO	Carry on
BOYFRIEND	'put your hands on me to know'
OLDER SISTER	'don't needta toucha to tell how you're feelin.'
BOYFRIEND	'Feel me and find out.'
O. SISTER EGO	No.
BOYFRIEND EGO	Good. Good. Nice. Nice.

OLDER SISTER	'You forgettin how much I know yer – '
O. SISTER EGO	good
OLDER SISTER	'you forgettin I got the gift a seein how you – knowin how you are, know how you are before you do, know you that well don't I.'
BOYFRIEND	'(I) know *you* that well, don't I? Girlfriend.'
OLDER SISTER	'Boyfriend.'
BOYFRIEND	
OLDER SISTER	
O. SISTER EGO	C'mon…
OLDER SISTER	
O. SISTER EGO	*Come on.*
OLDER SISTER	
O. SISTER EGO	He reminds me –
OLDER SISTER	'You remind me – '
BOYFRIEND	'what?'
O. SISTER EGO	He reminds me –
OLDER SISTER	'You remind me – '
BOYFRIEND	'what?'
OLDER SISTER	'You remind me of my dad.'
BOYFRIEND EGO	What?
O. SISTER EGO	Good.
BOYFRIEND	'What – dyin of it like he did?'
OLDER SISTER	'He didn't get that far.
	Beat.
	Did he.'
BOYFRIEND	'I'm not fightin / you – '

OLDER SISTER	'But Dad woulda offered.'
BOYFRIEND	'I'm offerin to care for you.'
O. SISTER EGO	Shit.
BOYFRIEND EGO	Nice. Nicely done.
OLDER SISTER	'Let me care for you.'
BOYFRIEND EGO	No.
BOYFRIEND	'I'd care for you good.'
O. SISTER EGO	Yeh right.
OLDER SISTER	'I'd care for you better.'
BOYFRIEND EGO	Yeh right.
BOYFRIEND	'You can't care as careful as I can. Can you?'
OLDER SISTER	
O. SISTER EGO	He'd care?
OLDER SISTER	'You'd care?'
BOYFRIEND	'I'd care.'
OLDER SISTER	'Do yer care?'
BOYFRIEND	'I care.'
OLDER SISTER	'How much?'
BOYFRIEND	'I care – '
OLDER SISTER	'more'n me?'
BOYFRIEND EGO	Yeh yeh
BOYFRIEND	'I care'
OLDER SISTER	'more'n me? It is more'n me'
BOYFRIEND EGO	yeh
OLDER SISTER	'you are better'n me then'
BOYFRIEND EGO	I'm better'n you –

OLDER SISTER	'if you can care that much'
BOYFRIEND EGO	I am better
OLDER SISTER	'you be well better / than – '
BOYFRIEND	'it's not about – '
BOYFRIEND EGO	it is – and I am.
OLDER SISTER	'If you're gonna be there and be that care – full.'
BOYFRIEND	'Well – '
BOYFRIEND EGO	I am / better.
O. SISTER EGO	See
BOYFRIEND	'I do care – '
OLDER SISTER	'do yer?'
BOYFRIEND	'I do – '
OLDER SISTER	'how much?'
BOYFRIEND EGO	Much.
BOYFRIEND	'Much.'
OLDER SISTER	'How much?'
BOYFRIEND EGO	Much.
O. SISTER EGO	More'n I know?
BOYFRIEND	'More'n you know.'
	OLDER SISTER EGO *smiles*.
OLDER SISTER	'As much as – '
BOYFRIEND EGO	more'n that
OLDER SISTER	'as much / as – '
BOYFRIEND	'more'n you could know babes'
BOYFRIEND EGO	see
OLDER SISTER	'as much as to let me have the prescription then?

As much as that…?

You can care as care – full as that?… As
full a care as that for me?
Can you?

Then let me have the prescription.

…Please.'

BOYFRIEND

BOYFRIEND

> OLDER SISTER EGO *smiles, triumphant.*

OLDER SISTER   'Meds for me.
Me caring for you.
I would.
I would.
I could. I could. I could.

Long pause.

My dad wouldn'ta (fought).
My dad wouldn'ta fought for it.
Dad wouldn'ta fought my mum for it.
Wouldn'ta made her, fight for it.'

BOYFRIEND

OLDER SISTER

BOYFRIEND

OLDER SISTER

> BOYFRIEND *carefully picks up the
prescription, then throws it on the ground
in front of* OLDER SISTER.

O. SISTER EGO

OLDER SISTER

> *Beat.*

OLDER SISTER

OLDER SISTER

BOYFRIEND EGO   She's right.

BOYFRIEND

BOYFRIEND EGO   She is better at it than me.

Fifteen

'*Stoning Mary.*'

OLDER SISTER

OLDER SISTER

CORR. OFFICER

OLDER SISTER

CORR. OFFICER   …You said you would…

OLDER SISTER

CORR. OFFICER   You know she asked you to.

I know she asked you to.

OLDER SISTER

OLDER SISTER

CORR. OFFICER   It's your sister. Bein stoned.

OLDER SISTER

CORR. OFFICER   And you promised / her.

OLDER SISTER   Have my ticket.

OLDER SISTER

OLDER SISTER   Take my ticket.

…I… don't wannit.

Sixteen

'Stoning Mary.'

(*The* CHILD SOLDIER*'s*) MUM *watches* MARY *for a while.*

MARY*'s head starts to be shaved down by the* CORRECTIONS OFFICER.

It rains.

MUM *picks up her first stone.*

End.

www.nickhernbooks.co.uk

facebook.com/nickhernbooks

twitter.com/nickhernbooks